Flood

Catherine Chambers

Heinemann Library

Chicago, Illinois

Designed by Visual Image
Illustration by Paul Bale
Originated by Ambassador Litho
Printed and bound in South China

06 05 04
10 9 8 7 6 5 4 3 2

Library of Congress Cataloging-in-Publication Data
Chambers, Catherine, 1954-
  Flood / Catherine Chambers.
      p. cm. -- (Wild weather)
Summary: Introduces what floods are, conditions that exist during floods, their harmful and beneficial effects, and their impact on humans, plants, and animals.
  ISBN 1-58810-655-1(HC), 1-4034-0112-8 (Pbk)
  1. Floods--Juvenile literature. [1. Floods.] I. Title. II. Series.
  GB1399 .C4797 2002
  551.48'9--dc21
                              2002000819

Acknowledgments
The author and publishers are grateful to the following for permission to reproduce copyright material: pp. 4, 8, 10, 12, 25, 29 Ecoscene; p. 5 Ardea; p. 7 Still Pictures; pp. 9, 11, 19 Oxford Scientific Films; pp. 13, 18 Reuters; pp 14, 16, 17, 23, 24, 28 Corbis; pp. 15, 20 Robert Harding Picture Library; pp. 21, 27 PA Photos; p. 22 EPA/PA photos; p. 26 Rex Features.

Cover photograph: Robert Harding Picture Library.

The publishers would like to thank the Met Office for their assistance with the preparation of this book.

Every effort has been made to contact copyright holders of any material reproduced in this book. Any omissions will be rectified in subsequent printings if notice is given to the publisher.

Some words are shown in bold, **like this.** You can find out what they mean by looking in the glossary.

Contents

What Is a Flood?

A flood happens when water covers land that is usually dry. Heavy rain makes river waters spill over their **banks.** Storms can make huge sea waves that flood the **coast.**

This city in North Dakota has been flooded by
the Red River. People have been forced to leave
their homes. The fields near the city have also
been flooded.

Where Do Floods Happen?

Floods happen most often in places where there are lots of storms. Storms bring heavy rain and strong winds. This can cause rivers to flood.

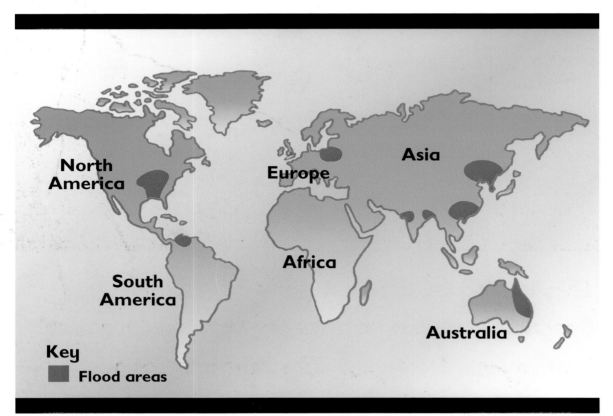

North America

Europe

Asia

Africa

South America

Australia

Key
Flood areas

This flood is in the country of Bangladesh. Bangladesh gets a lot of heavy rain from June to September. This time is called the monsoon season. Floods often happen in Bangladesh.

7

Heavy Rain

When winds blow over the oceans, they pick up tiny drops of **water vapor.** Cold air high in the sky cools the vapor into heavy drops of water. These drops fall as rain.

Clouds are made up of water vapor that has been cooled. Large, dark clouds hold a lot of water vapor. These clouds can bring heavy rain and sudden floods.

Why Do Floods Happen?

The flat land surrounding a river forms a **floodplain.** When heavy rain falls, the river can become too full. The water rises above the **banks** and spills onto the floodplain.

Strong winds often blow across the oceans during storms. They push the water into huge waves. These can rise over the shore and cause floods along the **coast.**

What Are Floods Like?

Sometimes floodwaters rise slowly. People have time to get ready for the flood. At other times floodwaters rise quickly. People and cars get caught in the flood.

The water soaks buildings and anything inside
them. Some things are washed away. The
water also brings a lot of dirt. The dirt has
been picked up by the floodwaters.

Mississippi River Floods

The town of Bellevue, Iowa, lies on the Mississippi River. When the river rises it often floods. **Flood defenses** have been built to try and stop the floods.

In 1993, there was a lot of rain. The river began
to rise over its **banks,** and the walls that were
built to stop the floods broke. The town flooded,
and many people had to leave their homes.

Harmful Floods

Floods can trap people and animals. They can cover roads and break bridges. During a flood, it can be harder to find fresh food to eat or clean water to drink.

Huge waves have flooded this **coast,** damaging boats and buildings. The roads have been covered in sand and stones. Fish, seabirds, and seaweed are washed up onto the shore.

Helpful Floods

Here in Bangladesh, plants rot in the water left by a flood. The rotted plants in the water help to make the soil **fertile.** Rice grows well in this soil.

A river flows very fast when there is a lot of rain. The fast river washes down a lot of mud. The mud settles on flooded fields. This can make the soil in these fields more fertile.

Preparing for Floods

Radio and television stations work with weather **forecasters** to warn people about floods. The most serious warning is the **flood alert.** This warns people that a flood is about to happen.

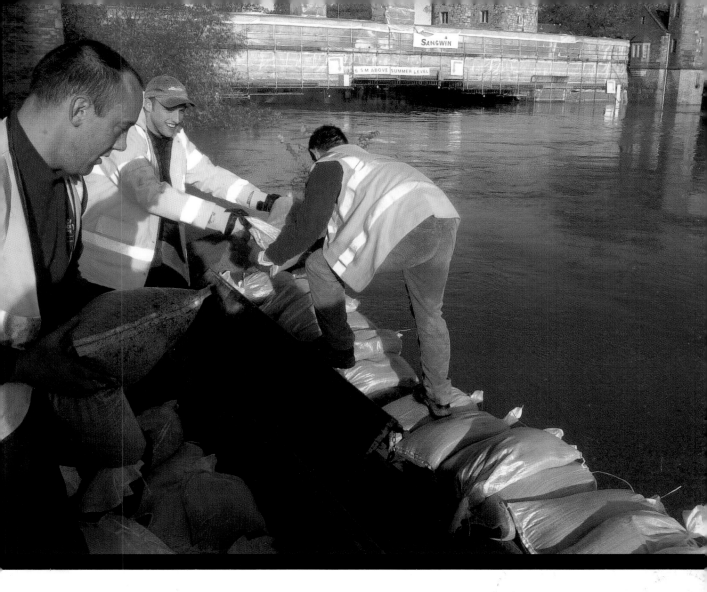

Before a flood, many people move their
furniture upstairs and switch off the electricity.
Sandbags stacked against doors can keep water
from getting in. Some people leave their homes.

Coping with Floods

In some countries there are bad floods nearly every year. So **flood shelters** are built on high ground. People hurry to these shelters when there is a flood.

Floodwaters can cover roads for many days.
Cars and buses cannot drive when the water is
high. People must travel by boat or by air.

Living with Floods

In areas that often flood, people build **platforms** on **stilts.** Cows, chickens, and other animals are kept safe on these platforms until the floodwaters go down.

Rice is a **crop** that grows in flooded fields, but heavy flooding destroys rice and other crops. They are battered by the flowing water. Then they rot in the ground.

To the Rescue!

The country of Mozambique was badly flooded in 2000. Helicopters rescued people from trees and high ground. They dropped food and equipment to make clean drinking water.

Lifeboats are being used to rescue these people from their flooded homes. The rescuers are taking the people to places that are above the flood. There they will find food and warmth.

Adapting to Floods

These houses are close to a river that often floods. The houses have been built on **stilts.** When the river floods, the houses will be above the floodwaters.

This is a new **dam** in the Netherlands. The dam's high walls keep the flat land below from being flooded. A road runs on top of the walls.

Fact File

◆ Scientists can learn about floods in the past by looking at tree rings. A tree adds a ring to its trunk every year. The ring for a flood year will look damaged.

◆ Earth's **climate** is changing all the time. Right now it seems to be getting hotter. This is called "global warming." Some scientists think that global warming will bring more floods.

◆ Cutting down trees can make floods worse. Soil can soak up rainwater like a sponge. But when there are no trees, the floodwaters wash away this soil. There is nothing left to soak up the water.

Glossary

bank high ground on either side of a river

climate normal weather in a part of the world

coast strip of land next to a large body of water

crop plant that is grown for food

dam wall that holds back water

fertile good for growing crops

flood alert last flood warning before rising waters get dangerous

flood defense barrier build to keep floodwaters from flowing onto the land

floodplain flat land near a river

flood shelter building on high ground where people can escape floods

forecaster someone who collects information about the weather in order to predict it

lifeboat boat for rescuing people from dangerous waters

platform flat floor raised above the ground

stilts tall poles that hold up platforms or buildings

water vapor water that has changed into a gas

More Books to Read

Ashwell, Miranda, and Andy Owen. *Rain*. Chicago: Heinemann Library, 1999.

Ashwell, Miranda, and Andy Owen. *Rivers*. Chicago: Heinemann Library, 1998.

Foster, Leila. *Asia*. Chicago: Heinemann Library, 2001.

Index